TRAVELS WITH TARRA
Carol Buckley

TILBURY HOUSE, PUBLISHERS

GARDINER, MAINE

When the baby Asian elephant arrived in America she was cold and hungry. Her trip from her home in Burma had taken nearly three days. She had been packed in a wooden crate with no windows, flying on a noisy, bumpy airplane. She was confused and frightened.

She could remember the comfort of standing underneath her mother's massive belly when suddenly all of the elephants in their herd started running in every direction. Somehow she got separated from her mother. The last thing she remembered was her mother and family trumpeting in alarm as the people dragged her away.

In California a man named Bob had ordered this baby elephant from an animal broker. In 1974 elephants were not protected and it was still legal to do this. The little elephant would be his pet but also a mascot for his tire stores. He hoped she would attract lots of business.

At the tire dealer's store, people from all over town came to see the elephant. Although she was three feet tall and weighed seven hundred pounds, she was still a baby, less than a year old. She had thick black hair covering her entire body. She looked very much like a prehistoric woolly mammoth.

Most of the children who came to see her had never seen a baby elephant before. Some teased her to prove how brave they were. They made a game of racing back and forth in front of her cage, just out of her reach. Thinking this was a game, she tried to run with them—but her cage was too small and she ran into its wall.

The children laughed at her. They didn't understand that she wanted to play with them. She became so unhappy that she did what any baby elephant would do—she opened her mouth and screamed. In a baby elephant's natural world this scream would bring her entire family to her side to comfort and protect her. But here the children ran away.

Bob made sure that the baby elephant was fed and watered and clean. Her cage had been built inside the back of a small delivery truck, making it easy for Bob to take her home with him each night after work. She soon learned the routine. Bob would drive home and park her truck in his driveway, turn on the heater, turn off the lights, and close the door for the night. But in the wild, baby elephants are never left alone—their family is always close by to protect and comfort them. She must have missed her mother's gentle touch and the security of her elephant relatives sleeping nearby.

I lived just a block away from Bob's Tire Store. One afternoon as I was doing my homework, my dog Tasha began barking. She was usually well behaved so I got up to investigate. I glanced out the window and almost fell over my desk trying to race out the front door.

There was a man walking a tiny baby elephant down my street! My heart was pounding. I had always liked working with animals, and at college I was studying about caring for exotic animals—but I had never been so close to a real elephant. I introduced myself and then couldn't believe my good fortune when Bob invited me to help feed her—anytime! He looked a bit surprised to see me waiting at the tire store when they returned from their walk a few minutes later.

Bob prepared her bottles and allowed me the thrill of feeding her the special baby elephant formula. It was a combination of powered milk, peanut butter, oatmeal, bananas, vitamins, and minerals all mixed together into a tasty drink. She lunged at the bottle with her mouth open and grabbed at it with her trunk. She sucked so hard I thought she would swallow the bottle, but instead she gulped the formula down in seconds. I gave her one bottle after another until she was full.

Then, with her tiny trunk she reached out for Bob's hand and pulled it in her mouth, thumb first. She dropped her head back and draped her limp trunk back over her face. Her long eyelashes fluttered slowly, her eyes closed, and she let out a heavy sigh. I heard what sounded like sucking.

Bob laughed and told me that she liked to suck his thumb after her bottles. Soon she let his hand drop from her mouth and then like a falling leaf gently dancing down from the sky, she folded ever so slowly to the floor and fell into a deep sleep.

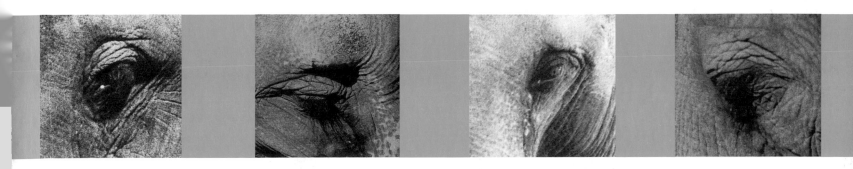

The tire store became my second home. Between school and sleep, I spent every moment with the baby elephant. After a few weeks Bob realized that I had become a permanent fixture at her cage so he gave me a job as her caretaker.

I started to read every book I could find about elephants. I learned that in the wild, a baby elephant would nurse from its mother for almost seven years but would also be eating some solid foods by now. Our local vet agreed that we should add different foods to her diet—fruit, vegetables, hay, and grain. I only had to show her once how to crack a watermelon open with her foot, and after that it was her favorite fruit!

After breakfast she would be ready to play. She thought it was great fun to pick up wood shavings with her trunk and throw them onto her back, sides, and belly. This dusting is a natural behavior that elephants do to protect their sensitive skin from biting insects and sunburn, but she wasn't concerned about skin care— she just liked to play. By the time she was done, not only was she covered from head to toe with shavings, but so was I.

When she tired of her play she would find a big pile of shavings and gently lie down in the middle of it to take a nap. Like most babies, she napped a lot.

As soon as she was asleep, I would leave for my next class. I thought sneaking off while she was asleep was a good idea, but if she awoke while I was gone, she was upset and sad. She had bonded to me and considered me to be her family. In the wild, her mother and sisters and aunts and cousins would always be with her, socializing and touching and taking care of each other. Here, she had me, but she still loved to touch and be touched. She would run her trunk over my clothes, arms, and shoes. Her favorite was my nose. Her trunk was tiny but strong. She would latch onto my nose and breathe. I soon realized that this was what elephants do when they greet one another. The difference was that my nose was very short.

I convinced Bob to let me to take the elephant home to my house each night so that we could be together in the evenings until we both went to sleep. She could get out of her truck and play in the grass in my back yard, scratch on a tree, and wallow in the dirt. Even a stick or a dried leaf became a perfect toy— she would grab it with her trunk, whisk it around in the air, chew on it, and then grind it under her tiny feet. Her play was fun to watch and showed me just how smart she was.

She also got to make friends with my dog Tasha. She loved Tasha at first sight. The last thing Tasha wanted was to let a baby elephant maul her from nose to tail, but that was how it was going to be. Because of Tasha, she would grow up loving dogs of all sizes and colors.

My school lunch break became our class time. I made her lessons short to keep her interested. She was so quick to learn that I had to work hard coming up with new and fun things for her each day.

First, she learned to hold a stick and strike the keys of a xylophone. She seemed to enjoy hearing the music and played without prompting. Her eyes would sparkle and she fluttered her eyelashes as I praised her new talents and gave her a treat. She learned to ring a bell, blow a whistle, and even beat on a drum, but what she seemed to enjoy the most was playing the harmonica. The children who came to see her were amazed how coordinated her trunk was. They were surprised that she could pick up the harmonica and position it correctly so that when she blew it made music. The more they giggled the louder she played!

It was also time for her to learn what are called stable manners. As you might guess, standing still was the most difficult one for this elephant. She learned to walk forward and backward when I asked her to. Even turning right and left seemed to be no problem. She quickly learned what the different words meant and loved to show off her lesson of the day. If I made a mistake myself, she would stop and glance over her shoulder at me with a devilish look as if to say, "What's wrong? Don't you know your right from your left?"

After we had been together for a few months, her manners improved. She learned many tricks that she enjoyed performing at parties, school bazaars, and even on television shows—she loved the attention she got by performing.

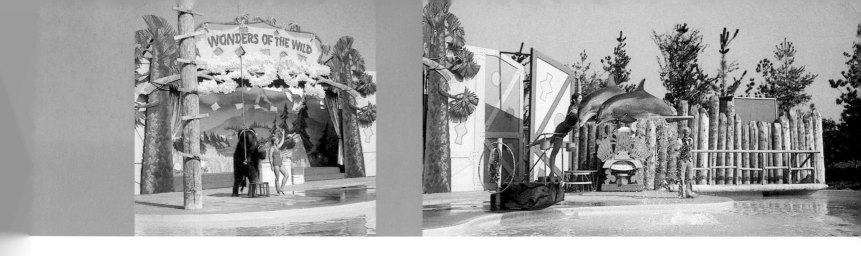

  The summer after her second birthday we took a job together at a theme park. The first thing I did was to give her a new name—Tarra (Tar-rah). Bob had called her Fluffie, but I thought her new name fit her better—it seemed exotic and grand, and I knew she would grow into it.

  Tarra was still so tiny many people who saw her in the show did not believe she was real. She moved through her routine with agility and ease, amazing the audience. Then, with a quick curtsy and a wave, she ran offstage anticipating her favorite part of the day—a shower. Tarra loved to roll around under the spray of the water and play in the puddles.

  There was something else fun in the water at this theme park—dolphins! The first time Tarra saw one she was standing close to the edge of their pool. The more curious of the two dolphins poked his face above the surface of the water just as Tarra was reaching her trunk down to splash. He surprised her, and she bellowed and bolted away, almost knocking me over. With encouragement Tarra worked up the confidence to approach the water's edge again. This same playful dolphin leaped out of the water and squirted water right at her. This time Tarra's squeals were ones of delight. For the remainder of the season it was hard keeping Tarra away from the edge of the dolphin pool.

  That summer was filled with many new adventures for the two of us. Our relationship grew stronger because we spent every moment of the day together.

All summer I had been trying to convince Bob to sell Tarra to me, and he finally agreed. Tarra would be mine to care for and protect for the rest of her life. The moment he said yes was the greatest feeling of happiness I could imagine.

Tarra and I worked for two years at the theme park, and then I decided to take Tarra on the road. I thought that traveling with a circus would be exciting for both of us.

I borrowed money from a bank and bought a special truck trailer with a living area for Tarra, a tack room for her food and props, and a living area for me. We would be together all of the time, day and night. We would even get to sleep in the same trailer! I knew Tarra would love it and she did.

At night she would wait to lie down until I was in bed, then she would settle in for the night—but not quietly. Instead of simply lying down she would lean against the wall as she slid down, making the trailer rock from side to side. When she was little it was not too bad, but as she grew it felt like the trailer was going to flip on its side. Once she was lying down it would take several minutes for her to get comfortable. She squirmed, bounced, and kicked her feet around. When she was finally comfortable, I could hear her give a big sigh. I always knew when she was asleep because the trailer was perfectly still—except for the loud snoring coming from Tarra's room.

What made our traveling enjoyable was the adventure of exploring nature while on the road. From California to New York and everywhere in between, we stopped at least once a day, just to play. Tarra was full of energy, so it was important for her to have the opportunity to run and play.

Tarra was growing rapidly, nearly ten inches taller each year! By the time she was six years old she was over five feet tall and weighed close to four thousand pounds. She began to change in other ways, too. Her old tricks seemed to bore her. I needed to find new ways to make the job fun—things she would enjoy that would also entertain the public.

Tarra's agility had always amazed me, so I decided to see if I could teach her to roller-skate. I had special skates made for her, and when I put the two front

skates on her for the first time, she started goofing around with them right away.
I stood back and watched as she taught herself to skate—she was a natural! Then
I strapped on the back skates and said, "Okay, go play." This is what I always said
just before she ran off to play with her dogs, splash in the creek, or throw herself
into a new pile of sand. "Go play" were the two words she lived for. Skating
became another playtime.

By the spring of 1981 Tarra was getting famous. Her picture was on the front page of the *Los Angeles Times* and the headlines read, "What has 16 wheels and a trunk? Tarra—the world's only roller-skating elephant."

Tarra was asked to display her skating talents in shows around the world. I went with Tarra everywhere. We even flew to Korea, to appear in an international stage show. She skated with the New York City Rockettes' chorus line in the opening ceremonies of the famous Thanksgiving Day Parade, and at the Academy Awards in Los Angeles, she walked across the stage to present the award envelope for the movie *Passage to India*. In the movie *Annie*, Tarra skated while comedienne Carol Burnett rode on her back.

Circuses also booked Tarra for their shows. Backstage at the circus was always busy prior to showtime as performers and the prop crew prepared for the show. Getting Tarra into her skates and wardrobe took a full thirty minutes. The entire time she chirped and squealed, eager to get on stage.

We knew it was showtime when the house lights fell and the band started playing a traditional circus theme. Then the announcer bellowed into the microphone, "Ladies and gentlemen, children of all ages: a marvel like you have never seen before, the graceful, the talented, the one and only Tarra—the world's only roller-skating elephant."

Dozens of spotlights darted around the stage, and then, with grace and power, Tarra burst through the curtain wearing a sequin-studded blanket bearing her name, a fancy headpiece, and chrome-plated skates with knee-high boots. The crowds had never seen anything like it—they went wild! Tarra seemed to feed off the noise and excitement, skating around the big track with her trunk and tail extended, chattering in excitement the entire time. I had a hard time keeping up with her!

As Tarra grew older, skating continued to be easy for her but it no longer held the thrill it had when she was younger. I decided she needed another change, so for the next five years we spent the summer months giving elephant rides at zoos across the United States, filming some television commercials, appearing on talk shows, and making guest appearances. This new lifestyle left more time for Tarra and me to spend at our small farm in a national forest. There was nothing but wilderness surrounding us, and accompanied by our dogs and a pet goat, Tarra was in elephant heaven. She climbed every hill, explored the woods, and swam in the nearby lake and river to her heart's content.

But at the end of the next summer's ride season we did not return home. Instead, we headed up to Canada, where I had a new job taking care of elephants at a zoo that had seven elephants. This was a dream come true for me. I had finally found a place where Tarra and I could still be together but where she could finally be with other elephants.

Tarra was curious at first about the other elephants, but one of them kept chasing her and picking on her, so when spring arrived we moved again. I had found a job in a small zoo in Wisconsin that had just one elephant. Her name was Rasha. She was an Asian elephant like Tarra, a year older, and had spent most of her captive life without other elephants.

Tarra and Rasha were afraid of each other at first but with a few words of encouragement, they approached and began to gently touch each other with their trunks. To my great joy, they became best friends—practically overnight. They slept side by side, and when I came into the barn in the mornings both elephants would dart around playfully, chirping, squealing, and trumpeting, flapping their ears so fast it looked as if they would fly. Rasha watched and imitated everything Tarra did. Tarra had never been more content.

Things went so well that the zoo decided to send both elephants to an animal park in Canada where there were male elephants. Tarra and Rasha were each old enough to have a baby and begin a family. When we arrived at the animal park Rasha showed no fear. She was anxious to interact with the other elephants and got along well with them, but two of the elephants picked on Tarra, who was miserable again.

Seeing Tarra this unhappy was sad for me. I wondered if she would ever be able to enjoy being with a herd of elephants. Rasha sensed that Tarra was upset and tried to help by spending time with her, but it didn't seem to make a difference. Tarra was afraid of all the elephants except Rasha.

The plan had been for Tarra and Rasha to remain at the animal park until both were pregnant and then we would return to the zoo. But the zoo decided it could no longer afford to maintain two elephants and returned Rasha to the zoo to live alone. This was a sad day for everyone. Rasha lost all of her elephant friends, and Tarra would miss her only elephant friend. I felt helpless knowing I couldn't prevent any of this from happening.

The day after Rasha left, we got some happier news: Tarra was pregnant. To make sure that Tarra remained healthy, I took her for walks every day. Another elephant keeper named Scott took an interest in Tarra. He bathed her, joined us on her daily walks, and soon gained her trust. Before long she was comfortable around Scott and considered him a friend, but she continued to avoid the other elephants so we moved to another zoo in preparation for the birth.

When it was finally time for Tarra to have her baby, we soon realized that something was wrong. The vet was helping Tarra, but the calf was stillborn, dead before she was even born. This often happens with first-time mother elephants in the wild, but I never imagined that Tarra would have a problem. She was young, in good physical condition, got lots of exercise, and she had a healthy diet. We later found out that Tarra had been bitten by a mosquito carrying a disease that affected the baby but not Tarra.

After the birth Tarra approached her calf, whom we had hoped to name Maya. She gently placed her trunk over the calf's mouth and softly blew into Maya's mouth in an effort to get her to breathe. When there was no response she placed her trunk over Maya's trunk and gently blew into her trunk, but Maya did not respond. Finally, after Tarra had done everything her instincts directed her to do, she accepted that her baby was dead. She lovingly touched Maya one last time and then walked away.

Scott and I set up cots and slept in Tarra's barn to keep her company and to grieve together. She stood close and found it reassuring to be able to reach out and touch us throughout the night. But even during this sad time Tarra kept her sense of humor. In the middle of the night she would quietly place small piles of hay on top of us as we slept. When we woke up she would be towering over us, squeaking her delight that we were awake. Her antics helped the healing process, which was as much for us as for her.

Over the next few months I began to worry about Tarra's future. What would happen to her if I was gone? Since she could live to be seventy years old, she might even outlive me. I knew she needed a different life, one that was more like the life she would have had with her family in the wild. She no longer liked performing every day. She was bored living in a small yard at a zoo.

I knew Tarra could not go back to the wild—but what about bringing the wild to her? I dreamed of a place where many elephants like Tarra, from zoos and circuses, could live together as a family. It would be a sanctuary for captive elephants, a place built just for them. I knew I had to make that dream come true.

Scott agreed to help, and we began searching for the perfect piece of land. We found it in Tennessee—800 acres, surrounded by lots of uninhabited land that would serve as a buffer to keep the elephants safe. This would not be a zoo or a theme park. There would be no visitors. It would be just for the elephants. We decided to call it the Elephant Sanctuary.

When Tarra first arrived at the Elephant Sanctuary, she was very excited. She ran from her trailer and stood towering over me. She barked and squealed and put her head down low so we were eye to eye. Then she blasted a trumpet noise so loud I had to cover my ears. She danced around, chirping and trumpeting, and then headed out into the pastures and woods to explore.

She quickly discovered that food was growing all around her—grasses, leaves, berries, and nuts. There were spring-fed ponds where she bathed and a creek where she played. It was perfect. All we needed were more elephants.

And they came! Barbara was the first elephant to join Tarra at the Sanctuary. Then came Jenny, who was especially needy of other elephants so Tarra responded kindly to her. Soon after came Shirley, Bunny, Sissy, and Winkie—all from zoos and circuses. They didn't feel crowded at the Sanctuary and could take their time getting to know one another. As I had hoped they all got along very well and within days were acting like a family. When one becomes frightened or concerned the others run to her side to comfort her. They range in age from fifty-five to twenty-eight, so Tarra remains the baby.

Tarra thrives on the attention and pampering from her older family members and they like having a youngster to care for. After twenty-eight years Tarra finally has a family, and I know that she will never be alone again.

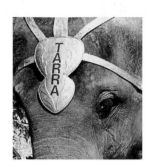
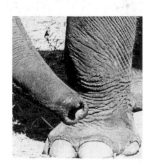
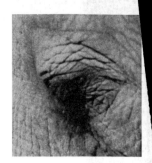

TILBURY HOUSE, PUBLISHERS
2 Mechanic Street • Gardiner, Maine 04345
800-582-1899 • www.tilburyhouse.com

First hardcover printing: May 2002
10 9 8 7 6 5 4 3 2 1

Library of Congress Cataloging-in-Publication Data
Buckley, Carol, 1954-
Travels with Tarra / Carol Buckley.
p. cm.
Summary: The author tells the story of the baby elephant
she raised, adopted, toured with in zoos and circuses, and
for which she eventually created a sanctuary.
ISBN 0-88448-241-3 (hardcover : alk. paper)
1. Asiatic elephant—United States—Biography—Juvenile
literature.
[1. Buckley, Carol, 1954- 2. Elephant trainers. 3. Women—
Biography. 4.
Asiatic elephant. 5. Elephants. 6. Wildlife refuges.] I. Title.
QL737.P98 B82 2002
599.67'6—dc21   2002001543

Production Credits
Editorial and production by Jennifer Elliott, Audrey
Maynard, and Barbara Diamond
Designed by Geraldine Millham, Westport, Massachusetts
Scanning by Integrated Composition Systems, Spokane,
Washington
Printing and binding by Worzalla Publishing, Stevens
Point, Wisconsin

Photo Credits
Ajay A. Desai, page 2; Krupakar Senani, pages 6–7;
Mildred Traeger, pages 10–11; Gary Phelps, pages 17,
21, 22, and 23; Seattle Post-Intelligencer, pages 26–27;
Michael Stadler, pages 38 and 39. All other photos
courtesy of the author.

CLASSROOM MATERIALS

Discovering Elephants: Classroom Materials for Teachers, from the Elephant Sanctuary, developed by J. L. Jones, Carol Buckley, and Scott Blais, is an outstanding classroom resource, full of information and activities. It's free, available for Grades K-3 and Grades 4–5, and can be easily downloaded from www.elephants.com

Project DIANE's Elephants on the Internet is an interactive video and multimedia teleconferencing program that provides an effective yet non-invasive opportunity for schools and the general public to visit the Sanctuary and experience the elephants "live" as they pursue their daily routine. For more about Project DIANE (Diversified Information and Assistance Network), visit the web site at www.diane.tnstate.edu.

http://www.elephants.com This is the Elephant Sanctuary's web site, which features photographs and information about Tarra and the other elephants, real-time viewing of the elephants at The Sanctuary, elephant curriculum materials that teachers can easily download, links to other sites about elephants, and much more. This is an wonderful website!

http://elephants.elehost.com The Elephant Information Repository is an extensive directory of elephant websites, organizations, events, etc.

http://hsus.org The Humane Society of the United States offers information about the treatment of captive animals and other issues.

http://www.elephant.tnet.co.th/ Friends of the Asian Elephant provides medical treatment and reintroduces elephants into the wild.

http://www.elephanttrust.org/cynthia-moss.htm Visit the web site of a world-leading expert on African elephant family structures, life cycle, and behavior and read about her work with elephants.